——Daily Cash Flo

Book No. [   ]   **Continued From Book No:** [   ]

Start Date: [   ]   **Department:** [   ]

Name:	
Position:	
Address:	
Business Address:	
Email:	
Telephone:	
Mobile:	
Fax:	

Notes:

Daily Cash Flow Log Book

| Sheet No. _____ | Month : _____ | Year : _____ |

| Date From: _____ To: _____ | Starting Balance: _____ |

Date	Description	Cash In	Cash Out	Balance
	Total			

| End Date: | Closing Balance: |

| Approved By: | Signature: |

Daily Cash Flow Log Book

Sheet No. _____	Month : _____	Year : _____

Date From: _____ To: _____	Starting Balance:_____

Date	Description	Cash In	Cash Out	Balance
Total				

End Date:	Closing Balance:

Approved By:	Signature:

Daily Cash Flow Log Book

| Sheet No. _____ | Month : _____ | Year : _____ |

| Date From: _____ To:_____ | Starting Balance:_____ |

Date	Description	Cash In	Cash Out	Balance
	Total			

| **End Date:** | **Closing Balance:** |

| **Approved By:** | **Signature:** |

Daily Cash Flow Log Book

| Sheet No. _____ | Month : _____ | Year : _____ |

| Date From: _____ To: _____ | Starting Balance: _____ |

Date	Description	Cash In	Cash Out	Balance
	Total			

| End Date: | Closing Balance: |

| Approved By: | Signature: |

Daily Cash Flow Log Book

Sheet No. _____   Month : _____   Year : _____

Date From: _____ To: _____   Starting Balance: _____

Date	Description	Cash In	Cash Out	Balance
Total				

End Date: Closing Balance:

Approved By: Signature:

Daily Cash Flow Log Book

| Sheet No. _____ | Month : _____ | Year : _____ |

| Date From: _____ To: _____ | Starting Balance:_____ |

Date	Description	Cash In	Cash Out	Balance
Total				

| End Date: | Closing Balance: |

| Approved By: | Signature: |

Daily Cash Flow Log Book

Sheet No. _____   Month : _____   Year : _____

Date From: _____ To: _____   Starting Balance: _____

Date	Description	Cash In	Cash Out	Balance
	Total			

End Date: _____   Closing Balance: _____

Approved By: _____   Signature: _____

Daily Cash Flow Log Book

| Sheet No. _____ | Month : _____ | Year : _____ |

| Date From: _____ To: _____ | Starting Balance: _____ |

Date	Description	Cash In	Cash Out	Balance
	Total			

| End Date: | Closing Balance: |

| Approved By: | Signature: |

Daily Cash Flow Log Book

| Sheet No. _____ | Month : _____ | Year : _____ |

| Date From: _____ To: _____ | Starting Balance: _____ |

Date	Description	Cash In	Cash Out	Balance
	Total			

| End Date: | Closing Balance: |

| Approved By: | Signature: |

Daily Cash Flow Log Book

| Sheet No. _____ | Month : _____ | Year : _____ |

| Date From: _____ To: _____ | Starting Balance: _____ |

Date	Description	Cash In	Cash Out	Balance
	Total			

| End Date: | Closing Balance: |

| Approved By: | Signature: |

Daily Cash Flow Log Book

Sheet No. _____   Month : _____   Year : _____

Date From: _____ To: _____   Starting Balance: _____

Date	Description	Cash In	Cash Out	Balance
	Total			

End Date: Closing Balance:

Approved By: Signature:

Daily Cash Flow Log Book

| Sheet No. _____ | Month : _____ | Year : _____ |

| Date From: _____ To: _____ | Starting Balance: _____ |

Date	Description	Cash In	Cash Out	Balance
Total				

| End Date: | Closing Balance: |

| Approved By: | Signature: |

Daily Cash Flow Log Book

Sheet No. _____ Month : _____ Year : _____

Date From: _____ To: _____   Starting Balance: _____

Date	Description	Cash In	Cash Out	Balance
	Total			

End Date: _____   Closing Balance: _____

Approved By: _____   Signature: _____

Daily Cash Flow Log Book

| Sheet No. _____ | Month : _____ | Year : _____ |

| Date From: _____ To: _____ | Starting Balance: _____ |

Date	Description	Cash In	Cash Out	Balance
	Total			

| End Date: | Closing Balance: |

| Approved By: | Signature: |

Daily Cash Flow Log Book

Sheet No. _____ Month : _____ Year : _____

Date From: _____ To: _____   Starting Balance: _____

Date	Description	Cash In	Cash Out	Balance
	Total			

End Date: Closing Balance:

Approved By: Signature:

Daily Cash Flow Log Book

Sheet No. _____	Month : _____	Year : _____

Date From: _____ To:_____	Starting Balance:_____

Date	Description	Cash In	Cash Out	Balance
	Total			

End Date:	Closing Balance:

Approved By:	Signature:

Daily Cash Flow Log Book

Sheet No. _____ | Month : _____ | Year : _____

Date From: _____ To: _____ | Starting Balance: _____

Date	Description	Cash In	Cash Out	Balance
	Total			

End Date: | Closing Balance:

Approved By: | Signature:

Daily Cash Flow Log Book

| Sheet No. _____ | Month : _____ | Year : _____ |

| Date From: _____ To: _____ | Starting Balance: _____ |

Date	Description	Cash In	Cash Out	Balance
	Total			

| End Date: | Closing Balance: |

| Approved By: | Signature: |

Daily Cash Flow Log Book

Sheet No. _____	Month : _____	Year : _____

Date From: _____ To: _____	Starting Balance: _____

Date	Description	Cash In	Cash Out	Balance
	Total			

End Date:	Closing Balance:

Approved By:	Signature:

Daily Cash Flow Log Book

| Sheet No. _____ | Month : _____ | Year : _____ |

| Date From: _____ To: _____ | Starting Balance: _____ |

Date	Description	Cash In	Cash Out	Balance
	Total			

| End Date: | Closing Balance: |

| Approved By: | Signature: |

Daily Cash Flow Log Book

Sheet No. _____   Month : _____   Year : _____

Date From: _____ To: _____   Starting Balance:_____

Date	Description	Cash In	Cash Out	Balance
	Total			

End Date: **Closing Balance:**

Approved By: **Signature:**

Daily Cash Flow Log Book

Sheet No. _____	Month : _____	Year : _____

Date From: _____ To: _____	Starting Balance: _____

Date	Description	Cash In	Cash Out	Balance
	Total			

End Date:	Closing Balance:

Approved By:	Signature:

Daily Cash Flow Log Book

Sheet No. _____	Month : _____	Year : _____

Date From: _____ To: _____	Starting Balance: _____

Date	Description	Cash In	Cash Out	Balance
	Total			

End Date:	Closing Balance:

Approved By:	Signature:

Daily Cash Flow Log Book

| Sheet No. _____ | Month : _____ | Year : _____ |

| Date From: _____ To: _____ | Starting Balance: _____ |

Date	Description	Cash In	Cash Out	Balance
Total				

| End Date: | Closing Balance: |

| Approved By: | Signature: |

Daily Cash Flow Log Book

| Sheet No. _____ | Month : _____ | Year : _____ |

| Date From: _____ To: _____ | Starting Balance: _____ |

Date	Description	Cash In	Cash Out	Balance
	Total			

| End Date: | Closing Balance: |

| Approved By: | Signature: |

Daily Cash Flow Log Book

Sheet No. _____	Month : _____	Year : _____

Date From: _____ To: _____	Starting Balance: _____

Date	Description	Cash In	Cash Out	Balance
	Total			

End Date:	Closing Balance:

Approved By:	Signature:

Daily Cash Flow Log Book

Sheet No. _____ Month : _____ Year : _____

Date From: _____ To: _____   Starting Balance: _____

Date	Description	Cash In	Cash Out	Balance
	Total			

End Date: _____   Closing Balance: _____

Approved By: _____   Signature: _____

Daily Cash Flow Log Book

Sheet No. _____   Month : _____   Year : _____

Date From: _____ To: _____   Starting Balance: _____

Date	Description	Cash In	Cash Out	Balance
	Total			

End Date: **Closing Balance:**

Approved By: **Signature:**

Daily Cash Flow Log Book

Sheet No. _____ Month : _____ Year : _____

Date From: _____ To: _____ Starting Balance: _____

Date	Description	Cash In	Cash Out	Balance
	Total			

End Date: _____ Closing Balance: _____

Approved By: Signature:

Daily Cash Flow Log Book

Sheet No. _____ Month : _____ Year : _____

Date From: _____ To: _____ Starting Balance: _____

Date	Description	Cash In	Cash Out	Balance
Total				

End Date: Closing Balance:

Approved By: Signature:

Daily Cash Flow Log Book

Sheet No. _____ Month : _____ Year : _____

Date From: _____ To:_____   Starting Balance:_____

Date	Description	Cash In	Cash Out	Balance
	Total			

End Date: _____   Closing Balance: _____

Approved By: _____ Signature: _____

Daily Cash Flow Log Book

Sheet No. _____	Month : _____	Year : _____

Date From: _____ To: _____	Starting Balance: _____

Date	Description	Cash In	Cash Out	Balance
	Total			

End Date:	Closing Balance:

Approved By:	Signature:

Daily Cash Flow Log Book

Sheet No. _____ Month : _____ Year : _____

Date From: _____ To: _____   Starting Balance: _____

Date	Description	Cash In	Cash Out	Balance
Total				

End Date: _____   Closing Balance: _____

Approved By: _____   Signature: _____

Daily Cash Flow Log Book

| Sheet No. _____ | Month : _____ | Year : _____ |

| Date From: _____ To: _____ | Starting Balance:_____ |

Date	Description	Cash In	Cash Out	Balance
	Total			

| End Date: | Closing Balance: |

| Approved By: | Signature: |

Daily Cash Flow Log Book

Sheet No. _____   Month : _____   Year : _____

Date From: _____ To: _____   Starting Balance: _____

Date	Description	Cash In	Cash Out	Balance
	Total			

End Date: Closing Balance:

Approved By: Signature:

Daily Cash Flow Log Book

Sheet No. _____ | Month : _____ | Year : _____

Date From: _____ To: _____ | Starting Balance: _____

Date	Description	Cash In	Cash Out	Balance
Total				

End Date: | Closing Balance:

Approved By: | Signature:

Daily Cash Flow Log Book

| Sheet No. _____ | Month : _____ | Year : _____ |

| Date From: _____ To: _____ | Starting Balance: _____ |

Date	Description	Cash In	Cash Out	Balance
	Total			

| End Date: | Closing Balance: |

| Approved By: | Signature: |

Daily Cash Flow Log Book

| Sheet No. _____ | Month : _____ | Year : _____ |

| Date From: _____ To: _____ | Starting Balance: _____ |

Date	Description	Cash In	Cash Out	Balance
Total				

| End Date: | Closing Balance: |

| Approved By: | Signature: |

Daily Cash Flow Log Book

Sheet No. _____ Month : _____ Year : _____

Date From: _____ To: _____ Starting Balance: _____

Date	Description	Cash In	Cash Out	Balance
	Total			

End Date: _____ Closing Balance: _____

Approved By: _____ Signature: _____

Daily Cash Flow Log Book

| Sheet No. _____ | Month : _____ | Year : _____ |

| Date From: _____ To:_____ | Starting Balance:_____ |

Date	Description	Cash In	Cash Out	Balance
Total				

| End Date: | Closing Balance: |

| Approved By: | Signature: |

Daily Cash Flow Log Book

| Sheet No. _____ | Month : _____ | Year : _____ |

| Date From: _____ To: _____ | Starting Balance: _____ |

Date	Description	Cash In	Cash Out	Balance
Total				

| **End Date:** | **Closing Balance:** |

| **Approved By:** | **Signature:** |

Daily Cash Flow Log Book

Sheet No. _____	Month : _____	Year : _____

Date From: _____ To: _____	Starting Balance: _____

Date	Description	Cash In	Cash Out	Balance
	Total			

End Date:	Closing Balance:
Approved By:	Signature:

Daily Cash Flow Log Book

Sheet No. _____	Month : _____	Year : _____

Date From: _____ To: _____	Starting Balance: _____

Date	Description	Cash In	Cash Out	Balance
	Total			

End Date:	Closing Balance:
Approved By:	**Signature:**

Daily Cash Flow Log Book

Sheet No. _____ Month : _____ Year : _____

Date From: _____ To:_____ Starting Balance:_____

Date	Description	Cash In	Cash Out	Balance
	Total			

End Date: _____ Closing Balance: _____

Approved By: _____ Signature: _____

Daily Cash Flow Log Book

Sheet No. _____   Month : _____   Year : _____

Date From: _____ To: _____   Starting Balance: _____

Date	Description	Cash In	Cash Out	Balance
	Total			

End Date: _____   Closing Balance: _____

Approved By: _____   Signature: _____

Daily Cash Flow Log Book

Sheet No. _____   Month : _____   Year : _____

Date From: _____ To: _____   Starting Balance: _____

Date	Description	Cash In	Cash Out	Balance
	Total			

End Date: _____   Closing Balance: _____

Approved By: _____   Signature: _____

Daily Cash Flow Log Book

Sheet No. _____   Month : _____   Year : _____

Date From: _____ To: _____   Starting Balance: _____

Date	Description	Cash In	Cash Out	Balance
	Total			

End Date: _____   Closing Balance: _____

Approved By: _____   Signature: _____

Daily Cash Flow Log Book

| Sheet No. _____ | Month : _____ | Year : _____ |

| Date From: _____ To: _____ | Starting Balance: _____ |

Date	Description	Cash In	Cash Out	Balance
Total				

| End Date: | Closing Balance: |

| Approved By: | Signature: |

Daily Cash Flow Log Book

Sheet No. _____   Month : _____   Year : _____

Date From: _____ To: _____   Starting Balance: _____

Date	Description	Cash In	Cash Out	Balance
	Total			

End Date: _____   **Closing Balance:** _____

Approved By: _____   **Signature:** _____

Daily Cash Flow Log Book

| Sheet No. _____ | Month : _____ | Year : _____ |

| Date From: _____ To: _____ | Starting Balance: _____ |

Date	Description	Cash In	Cash Out	Balance
	Total			

| End Date: | Closing Balance: |

| Approved By: | Signature: |

Daily Cash Flow Log Book

| Sheet No. _____ | Month : _____ | Year : _____ |

| Date From: _____ To: _____ | Starting Balance: _____ |

Date	Description	Cash In	Cash Out	Balance
	Total			

| End Date: | Closing Balance: |

| Approved By: | Signature: |

Daily Cash Flow Log Book

| Sheet No. _____ | Month : _____ | Year : _____ |

| Date From: _____ To: _____ | Starting Balance: _____ |

Date	Description	Cash In	Cash Out	Balance
	Total			

| End Date: | Closing Balance: |

| Approved By: | Signature: |

Daily Cash Flow Log Book

Sheet No. _____ Month : _____ Year : _____

Date From: _____ To:_____   Starting Balance:_____

Date	Description	Cash In	Cash Out	Balance
	Total			

End Date: _____   **Closing Balance:** _____

Approved By: _____   **Signature:** _____

Daily Cash Flow Log Book

| Sheet No. _____ | Month : _____ | Year : _____ |

| Date From: _____ To: _____ | Starting Balance: _____ |

Date	Description	Cash In	Cash Out	Balance
Total				

| End Date: | Closing Balance: |

| Approved By: | Signature: |

Daily Cash Flow Log Book

| Sheet No. _____ | Month : _____ | Year : _____ |

| Date From: _____ To: _____ | Starting Balance: _____ |

Date	Description	Cash In	Cash Out	Balance
	Total			

| End Date: | Closing Balance: |

| Approved By: | Signature: |

Daily Cash Flow Log Book

| Sheet No. _____ | Month : _____ | Year : _____ |

| Date From: _____ To: _____ | Starting Balance: _____ |

Date	Description	Cash In	Cash Out	Balance
	Total			

| End Date: | Closing Balance: |

| Approved By: | Signature: |

Daily Cash Flow Log Book

Sheet No. _____ Month : _____ Year : _____

Date From: _____ To: _____   Starting Balance: _____

Date	Description	Cash In	Cash Out	Balance
Total				

End Date: _____   Closing Balance: _____

Approved By: _____   Signature: _____

Daily Cash Flow Log Book

| Sheet No. _____ | Month : _____ | Year : _____ |

| Date From: _____ To: _____ | Starting Balance: _____ |

Date	Description	Cash In	Cash Out	Balance
Total				

| End Date: | Closing Balance: |
| Approved By: | Signature: |

Daily Cash Flow Log Book

| Sheet No. _____ | Month : _____ | Year : _____ |

| Date From: _____ To: _____ | Starting Balance: _____ |

Date	Description	Cash In	Cash Out	Balance
	Total			

| End Date: | Closing Balance: |

| Approved By: | Signature: |

Daily Cash Flow Log Book

Sheet No. _____   Month : _____   Year : _____

Date From: _____ To: _____   Starting Balance: _____

Date	Description	Cash In	Cash Out	Balance
Total				

End Date: _____   Closing Balance: _____

Approved By: _____   Signature: _____

Daily Cash Flow Log Book

Sheet No. _____ | Month : _____ | Year : _____

Date From: _____ To: _____ | Starting Balance: _____

Date	Description	Cash In	Cash Out	Balance
Total				

End Date: | Closing Balance:

Approved By: | Signature:

Daily Cash Flow Log Book

Sheet No. _____ | Month : _____ | Year : _____

Date From: _____ To:_____ | Starting Balance:_____

Date	Description	Cash In	Cash Out	Balance
Total				

End Date: | Closing Balance:

Approved By: | Signature:

Daily Cash Flow Log Book

| Sheet No. _____ | Month : _____ | Year : _____ |

| Date From: _____ To: _____ | Starting Balance:_____ |

Date	Description	Cash In	Cash Out	Balance
	Total			

| End Date: | Closing Balance: |

| Approved By: | Signature: |

Daily Cash Flow Log Book

Sheet No. _____	Month : _____	Year : _____

Date From: _____ To:_____	Starting Balance:_____

Date	Description	Cash In	Cash Out	Balance
Total				

End Date:	Closing Balance:
Approved By:	**Signature:**

Daily Cash Flow Log Book

| Sheet No. _____ | Month : _____ | Year : _____ |

| Date From: _____ To:_____ | Starting Balance: _____ |

Date	Description	Cash In	Cash Out	Balance
	Total			

| End Date: | Closing Balance: |

| Approved By: | Signature: |

Daily Cash Flow Log Book

Sheet No. _____	Month : _____	Year : _____

Date From: _____ To: _____	Starting Balance: _____

Date	Description	Cash In	Cash Out	Balance
	Total			

End Date:	Closing Balance:
Approved By:	Signature:

Daily Cash Flow Log Book

Sheet No. _____	Month : _____	Year : _____

Date From: _____ To: _____	Starting Balance: _____

Date	Description	Cash In	Cash Out	Balance
	Total			

End Date:	Closing Balance:

Approved By:	Signature:

Daily Cash Flow Log Book

Sheet No. _____ Month : _____ Year : _____

Date From: _____ To: _____ Starting Balance: _____

Date	Description	Cash In	Cash Out	Balance
Total				

End Date: _____ Closing Balance: _____

Approved By: _____ Signature: _____

Daily Cash Flow Log Book

| Sheet No. _____ | Month : _____ | Year : _____ |

| Date From: _____ To: _____ | Starting Balance: _____ |

Date	Description	Cash In	Cash Out	Balance
	Total			

| End Date: | Closing Balance: |

| Approved By: | Signature: |

Daily Cash Flow Log Book

| Sheet No. _____ | Month : _____ | Year : _____ |

| Date From: _____ To: _____ | Starting Balance: _____ |

Date	Description	Cash In	Cash Out	Balance
	Total			

| End Date: | Closing Balance: |

| Approved By: | Signature: |

Daily Cash Flow Log Book

Sheet No. _____	Month : _____	Year : _____

Date From: _____ To: _____	Starting Balance: _____

Date	Description	Cash In	Cash Out	Balance
	Total			

End Date:	Closing Balance:
Approved By:	**Signature:**

Daily Cash Flow Log Book

| Sheet No. _____ | Month : _____ | Year : _____ |

| Date From: _____ To: _____ | Starting Balance: _____ |

Date	Description	Cash In	Cash Out	Balance
	Total			

| End Date: | Closing Balance: |

| Approved By: | Signature: |

Daily Cash Flow Log Book

Sheet No. _____ | Month : _____ | Year : _____

Date From: _____ To: _____ | Starting Balance: _____

Date	Description	Cash In	Cash Out	Balance
	Total			

End Date: | Closing Balance:

Approved By: | Signature:

Daily Cash Flow Log Book

Sheet No. _____	Month : _____	Year : _____

Date From: _____ To: _____	Starting Balance: _____

Date	Description	Cash In	Cash Out	Balance
Total				

End Date:	Closing Balance:

Approved By:	Signature:

Daily Cash Flow Log Book

Sheet No. _____   Month : _____   Year : _____

Date From: _____ To:_____   Starting Balance:_____

Date	Description	Cash In	Cash Out	Balance
Total				

End Date: **Closing Balance:**

Approved By: **Signature:**

Daily Cash Flow Log Book

Sheet No. _____	Month : _____	Year : _____

Date From: _____ To: _____	Starting Balance: _____

Date	Description	Cash In	Cash Out	Balance
Total				

End Date:	Closing Balance:

Approved By:	Signature:

Daily Cash Flow Log Book

Sheet No. _____ Month : _____ Year : _____

Date From: _____ To: _____   Starting Balance: _____

Date	Description	Cash In	Cash Out	Balance
	Total			

End Date: _____   Closing Balance: _____

Approved By: _____   Signature: _____

Daily Cash Flow Log Book

Sheet No. _____   Month : _____   Year : _____

Date From: _____ To: _____   Starting Balance: _____

Date	Description	Cash In	Cash Out	Balance
Total				

End Date: Closing Balance:

Approved By: Signature:

Daily Cash Flow Log Book

| Sheet No. _____ | Month : _____ | Year : _____ |

| Date From: _____ To: _____ | Starting Balance: _____ |

Date	Description	Cash In	Cash Out	Balance
	Total			

| End Date: | Closing Balance: |

| Approved By: | Signature: |

Daily Cash Flow Log Book

Sheet No. _____ Month : _____ Year : _____

Date From: _____ To:_____ Starting Balance:_____

Date	Description	Cash In	Cash Out	Balance
Total				

End Date: Closing Balance:

Approved By: Signature:

Daily Cash Flow Log Book

Sheet No. _____ Month : _____ Year : _____

Date From: _____ To: _____ Starting Balance: _____

Date	Description	Cash In	Cash Out	Balance
	Total			

End Date: _____ Closing Balance: _____

Approved By: _____ Signature: _____

Daily Cash Flow Log Book

Sheet No. _____ | Month : _____ | Year : _____

Date From: _____ To: _____ | Starting Balance: _____

Date	Description	Cash In	Cash Out	Balance
Total				

End Date: | Closing Balance:

Approved By: | Signature:

Daily Cash Flow Log Book

Sheet No. _____ Month : _____ Year : _____

Date From: _____ To: _____   Starting Balance: _____

Date	Description	Cash In	Cash Out	Balance
	Total			

End Date: _____   Closing Balance: _____

Approved By: _____   Signature: _____

Daily Cash Flow Log Book

Sheet No. _____ Month : _____ Year : _____

Date From: _____ To: _____ Starting Balance: _____

Date	Description	Cash In	Cash Out	Balance
Total				

End Date: _____ Closing Balance: _____

Approved By: _____ Signature: _____

Daily Cash Flow Log Book

Sheet No. _____ Month : _____ Year : _____

Date From: _____ To: _____   Starting Balance: _____

Date	Description	Cash In	Cash Out	Balance
	Total			

End Date: Closing Balance:

Approved By: Signature:

Daily Cash Flow Log Book

Sheet No. _____	Month : _____	Year : _____

Date From: _____ To: _____	Starting Balance: _____

Date	Description	Cash In	Cash Out	Balance
Total				

End Date:	Closing Balance:

Approved By:	Signature:

Daily Cash Flow Log Book

Sheet No. _____   Month : _____   Year : _____

Date From: _____ To: _____   Starting Balance: _____

Date	Description	Cash In	Cash Out	Balance
	Total			

End Date: _____   Closing Balance: _____

Approved By: _____   Signature: _____

Daily Cash Flow Log Book

Sheet No. _____ Month : _____ Year : _____

Date From: _____ To: _____   Starting Balance: _____

Date	Description	Cash In	Cash Out	Balance
	Total			

End Date: Closing Balance:

Approved By: Signature:

Daily Cash Flow Log Book

Sheet No. _____ | Month : _____ | Year : _____

Date From: _____ To: _____ | Starting Balance: _____

Date	Description	Cash In	Cash Out	Balance
	Total			

End Date: _____ | Closing Balance: _____

Approved By: _____ | Signature: _____

Daily Cash Flow Log Book

Sheet No. _____   Month : _____   Year : _____

Date From: _____ To: _____   Starting Balance: _____

Date	Description	Cash In	Cash Out	Balance
	Total			

End Date: Closing Balance:

Approved By: Signature:

Daily Cash Flow Log Book

| Sheet No. _____ | Month : _____ | Year : _____ |

| Date From: _____ To: _____ | Starting Balance: _____ |

Date	Description	Cash In	Cash Out	Balance
	Total			

| End Date: | Closing Balance: |

| Approved By: | Signature: |

Daily Cash Flow Log Book

Sheet No. _____ Month : _____ Year : _____

Date From: _____ To:_____   Starting Balance:_____

Date	Description	Cash In	Cash Out	Balance
	Total			

End Date: _____   Closing Balance:_____

Approved By: _____   Signature: _____

Daily Cash Flow Log Book

Sheet No. _____	Month : _____	Year : _____

Date From: _____ To: _____	Starting Balance: _____

Date	Description	Cash In	Cash Out	Balance
	Total			

End Date:	Closing Balance:

Approved By:	Signature:

Daily Cash Flow Log Book

Sheet No. _____	Month : _____	Year : _____

Date From: _____ To: _____	Starting Balance: _____

Date	Description	Cash In	Cash Out	Balance
Total				

End Date:	Closing Balance:
Approved By:	Signature:

Daily Cash Flow Log Book

Sheet No. _____ Month : _____ Year : _____

Date From: _____ To: _____ Starting Balance: _____

Date	Description	Cash In	Cash Out	Balance
	Total			

End Date: _____ Closing Balance: _____

Approved By: _____ Signature: _____

Daily Cash Flow Log Book

Sheet No. _____ Month : _____ Year : _____

Date From: _____ To: _____ Starting Balance: _____

Date	Description	Cash In	Cash Out	Balance
Total				

End Date: _____ Closing Balance: _____

Approved By: _____ Signature: _____

Daily Cash Flow Log Book

Sheet No. _____ Month : _____ Year : _____

Date From: _____ To: _____   Starting Balance: _____

Date	Description	Cash In	Cash Out	Balance
Total				

End Date: _____   Closing Balance: _____

Approved By: Signature:

Daily Cash Flow Log Book

Sheet No. _____   Month : _____   Year : _____

Date From: _____ To: _____   Starting Balance: _____

Date	Description	Cash In	Cash Out	Balance
Total				

End Date: Closing Balance:

Approved By: Signature:

Daily Cash Flow Log Book

Sheet No. _____   Month : _____   Year : _____

Date From: _____ To: _____   Starting Balance: _____

Date	Description	Cash In	Cash Out	Balance
Total				

End Date: _____   Closing Balance: _____

Approved By: _____   Signature: _____

Daily Cash Flow Log Book

Sheet No. _____ Month : _____ Year : _____

Date From: _____ To: _____   Starting Balance: _____

Date	Description	Cash In	Cash Out	Balance
Total				

End Date: _____   Closing Balance: _____

Approved By: _____   Signature: _____

Daily Cash Flow Log Book

Sheet No. _____   Month : _____   Year : _____

Date From: _____ To: _____   Starting Balance: _____

Date	Description	Cash In	Cash Out	Balance
Total				

End Date: _____   Closing Balance: _____

Approved By: _____   Signature: _____

Daily Cash Flow Log Book

| Sheet No. _____ | Month : _____ | Year : _____ |

| Date From: _____ To: _____ | Starting Balance: _____ |

Date	Description	Cash In	Cash Out	Balance
Total				

| End Date: | Closing Balance: |

| Approved By: | Signature: |

Daily Cash Flow Log Book

Sheet No. _____ Month : _____ Year : _____

Date From: _____ To: _____   Starting Balance: _____

Date	Description	Cash In	Cash Out	Balance
	Total			

End Date: _____   Closing Balance: _____

Approved By: _____   Signature: _____

Daily Cash Flow Log Book

| Sheet No. _____ | Month : _____ | Year : _____ |

| Date From: _____ To: _____ | Starting Balance: _____ |

Date	Description	Cash In	Cash Out	Balance
	Total			

| End Date: | Closing Balance: |

| Approved By: | Signature: |

Daily Cash Flow Log Book

Sheet No. _____ Month : _____ Year : _____

Date From: _____ To: _____ Starting Balance: _____

Date	Description	Cash In	Cash Out	Balance
	Total			

End Date: _____ Closing Balance: _____

Approved By: _____ Signature: _____

Daily Cash Flow Log Book

Sheet No. _____   Month : _____   Year : _____

Date From: _____ To: _____   Starting Balance: _____

Date	Description	Cash In	Cash Out	Balance
Total				

End Date: **Closing Balance:**

Approved By: **Signature:**

Daily Cash Flow Log Book

Sheet No. _____ | Month : _____ | Year : _____

Date From: _____ To: _____ | Starting Balance: _____

Date	Description	Cash In	Cash Out	Balance
	Total			

End Date: | Closing Balance:

Approved By: | Signature:

Daily Cash Flow Log Book

| Sheet No. _____ | Month : _____ | Year : _____ |

| Date From: _____ To: _____ | Starting Balance: _____ |

Date	Description	Cash In	Cash Out	Balance
	Total			

| End Date: | Closing Balance: |

| Approved By: | Signature: |

Made in United States
Troutdale, OR
07/13/2024

21201232R00064